HOLIDAY FUN

JUNETEENTH

KIM THOMPSON

NORWOOD HOUSE PRESS

Cataloging-in-Publication Data

Names: Thompson, Kim.
Title: Juneteenth / Kim Thompson.
Description: Buffalo, NY : Norwood House Press, 2027. | Series: Holiday fun | Includes glossary and index.
Identifiers: ISBN 9781978580688 (pbk.) | ISBN 9781978580695 (library bound) | ISBN 9781978580701 (ebook)
Subjects: LCSH: Juneteenth--Juvenile literature. | African Americans--Texas--History--Juvenile literature. | Enslaved persons--Emancipation--United States--Juvenile literature. | African Americans--Anniversaries, etc.--Juvenile literature.
Classification: LCC E185.93.T4 T548 2027 | DDC 394.263--dc23

Published in 2027 by
Norwood House Press
2544 Clinton Street
Buffalo, NY 14224

Designer: Rhea Magaro
Editor: Tricia Hoffman

Photo credits: Cover, p. 1 Lightspring/Shutterstock.com; p. 5 William A. Morgan/Shutterstock.com; p. 6 Wikipedia; p. 7 Morphart Creations inc./Shutterstock.com; pp. 9, 10, 11, 19 Library of Congress; p. 12 PenWin/Shutterstock.com; p. 13 Wirestock Creators/Shutterstock.com; p. 15 Sheila Fitzgerald/Shutterstock.com; p. 16 BEAMBER/Shutterstock.com; p. 17 FoodVideoPhoto/Shutterstock.com; p. 18 The Library Company of Philadelphia; p. 21 Aaron of L.A. Photography/Shutterstock.com;

Printed in the United States of America

CPSIA compliance information: Batch #CSNHP27: For further information contact Norwood House Press at 1-800-237-9932.

TABLE OF CONTENTS

JUNETEENTH IS HERE!

There is a big cookout. You sip strawberry soda. A band plays the **blues**.

On this **holiday**, people celebrate being free. It is Juneteenth!

A SPECIAL DAY

The Civil War ended in March 1865. The North won. The South lost.

Slavery was not legal. But some white people in Texas did not obey the law.

On June 19th, Northern soldiers went to Texas. They read the law out loud. They let Black people know they were free.

Black people **rejoiced**. They could do what they wanted. They could earn money.

A few of them bought some land. They made it into a park. They had a party there every year on June 19th.

Soon, many Black people celebrated Juneteenth. In 2021, it became an **official** holiday for all Americans. It comes every year on June 19th.

CHAMPION

HOW TO CELEBRATE

People go to church. Families have **reunions**.

There are parties and parades. People play music and dance.

SFPD
Shakespeare Company
HONORING
OUR PAST
INSPIRING
OUR FUTURE
JUNETEENTH

Red stands for **sacrifice**. People eat red foods. There are red beans and red velvet cake. There are watermelons and strawberries.

People read the **Emancipation Proclamation**. It says, “All persons held as slaves...shall be...forever free.”

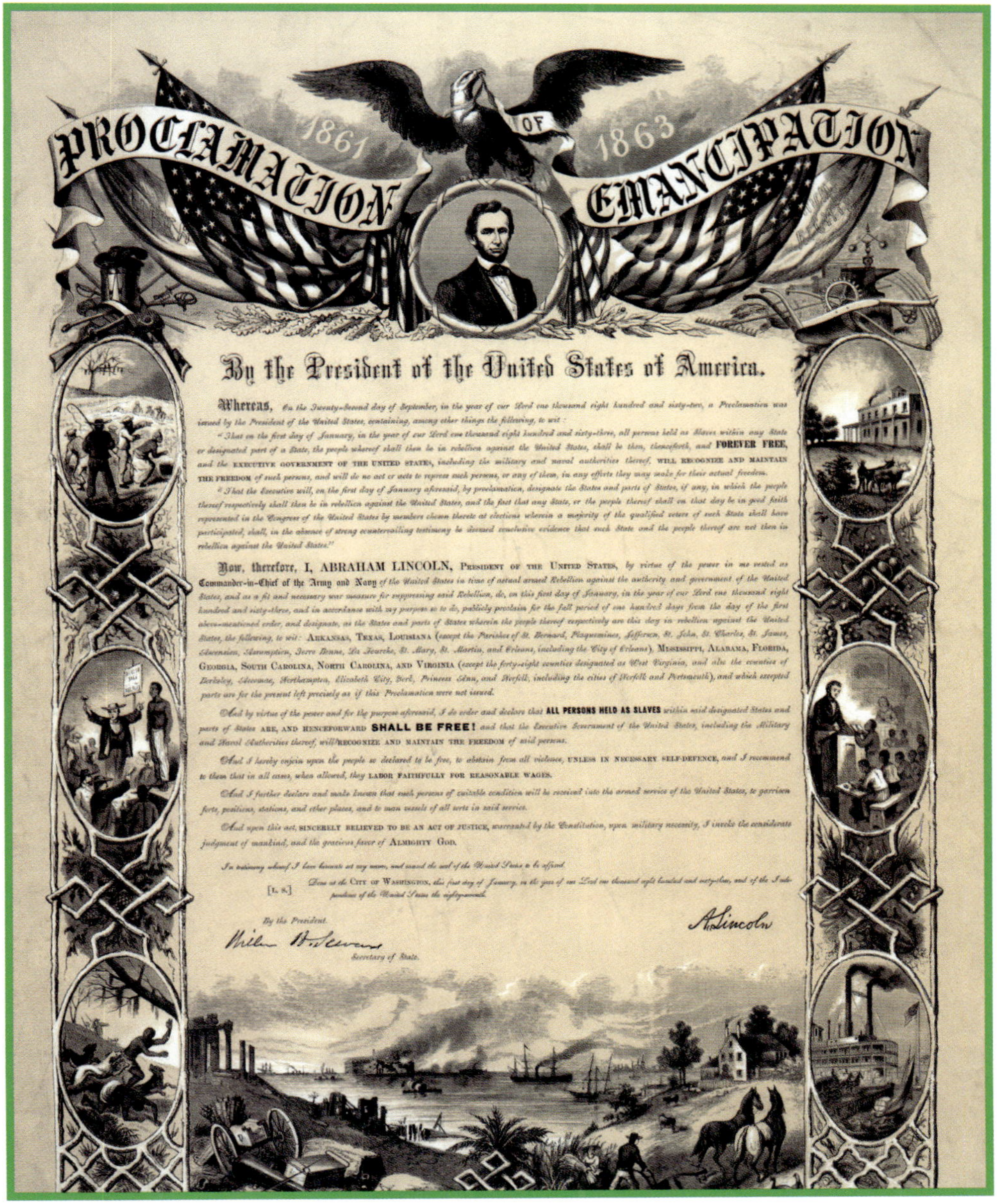

PROCLAMATION 1861 OF 1863 EMANCIPATION

By the President of the United States of America.

Whereas, On the Twenty-Second day of September, in the year of our Lord one thousand eight hundred and sixty-two, a Proclamation was issued by the President of the United States, containing, among other things the following, to wit:

"That on the first day of January, in the year of our Lord one thousand eight hundred and sixty-three, all persons held as Slaves within any State or designated part of a State, the people whereof shall then be in rebellion against the United States, shall be then, thenceforth, and **FOREVER FREE,** and the EXECUTIVE GOVERNMENT OF THE UNITED STATES, including the military and naval authorities thereof, WILL RECOGNIZE AND MAINTAIN THE FREEDOM of such persons, and will do no act or acts to repress such persons, or any of them, in any efforts they may make for their actual freedom.

"That the Executive will, on the first day of January aforesaid, by proclamation, designate the States and parts of States, if any, in which the people thereof respectively shall then be in rebellion against the United States, and the fact that any State, or the people thereof shall on that day be in good faith represented in the Congress of the United States by members chosen thereto at elections wherein a majority of the qualified voters of such State shall have participated, shall, in the absence of strong countervailing testimony be deemed conclusive evidence that such State and the people thereof are not then in rebellion against the United States."

Now, therefore, I, ABRAHAM LINCOLN, PRESIDENT OF THE UNITED STATES, by virtue of the power in me vested as **Commander-in-Chief of the Army and Navy** of the United States in time of actual armed Rebellion against the authority and government of the United States, and as a fit and necessary war measure for suppressing said Rebellion, do, on this first day of January, in the year of our Lord one thousand eight hundred and sixty-three, and in accordance with my purpose so to do, publicly proclaim for the full period of one hundred days from the day of the first above-mentioned order, and designate, as the States and parts of States wherein the people thereof respectively are this day in rebellion against the United States, the following, to wit: ARKANSAS, TEXAS, LOUISIANA (except the Parishes of St. Bernard, Plaquemines, Jefferson, St. John, St. Charles, St. James, Ascension, Assumption, Terre Bonne, La Fourche, St. Mary, St. Martin, and Orleans, including the City of Orleans), MISSISSIPPI, ALABAMA, FLORIDA, GEORGIA, SOUTH CAROLINA, NORTH CAROLINA, AND VIRGINIA (except the forty-eight counties designated as West Virginia, and also the counties of Berkeley, Accomac, Northampton, Elizabeth City, York, Princess Ann, and Norfolk, including the cities of Norfolk and Portsmouth), and which excepted parts are for the present left precisely as if this Proclamation were not issued.

And by virtue of the power and for the purpose aforesaid, I do order and declare that **ALL PERSONS HELD AS SLAVES** within said designated States and parts of States ARE, AND HENCEFORWARD **SHALL BE FREE!** and that the Executive Government of the United States, including the Military and Naval Authorities thereof, will RECOGNIZE AND MAINTAIN THE FREEDOM of said persons.

And I hereby enjoin upon the people so declared to be free, to abstain from all violence, UNLESS IN NECESSARY SELF-DEFENCE, and I recommend to them that in all cases, when allowed, they LABOR FAITHFULLY FOR REASONABLE WAGES.

And I further declare and make known that such persons of suitable condition will be received into the armed service of the United States, to garrison forts, positions, stations, and other places, and to man vessels of all sorts in said service.

And upon this act, SINCERELY BELIEVED TO BE AN ACT OF JUSTICE, warranted by the Constitution, upon military necessity, I invoke the considerate judgment of mankind, and the gracious favor of ALMIGHTY GOD.

In testimony whereof I have hereunto set my name, and caused the seal of the United States to be affixed.

[L. S.] Done at the CITY OF WASHINGTON, this first day of January, in the year of our Lord one thousand eight hundred and sixty-three, and of the Independence of the United States the eighty-seventh.

A. Lincoln

By the President.

William H. Seward
Secretary of State.

On Juneteenth, people honor the end of slavery.

Everyone is free, and everyone is happy!

DAZED
REMEMBERING MY ANCESTORS

GLOSSARY

blues (blooz): a type of music first sung by African Americans about the hardships of life

Emancipation Proclamation (i-MAN-suh-pay-shuhn prah-kluh-MAY-shuhn): an order given by President Abraham Lincoln in 1863 that said all enslaved people in the South were free

holiday (HAH-li-day): a special day; a day when most people do not go to school or work because of a religious or national celebration

official (uh-FISH-uhl): decided by people with authority; by law

rejoiced (ri-JOISD): felt great joy and happiness

reunions (ree-YOON-yuhnz): meetings of people who have not seen each other for a long time

sacrifice (SAK-ruh-fise): suffering and giving up things you value

slavery (SLAY-vur-ee): a system in which people are kidnapped, kept against their will, and made to work without pay or rights; slavery of Black people was legal in the United States before the Civil War

THINKING QUESTIONS

1. When is Juneteenth?
2. Why did Northern soldiers go to Texas in 1865?
3. Where was the first Juneteenth celebration?
4. Why is red food eaten on Juneteenth?
5. What does the Emancipation Proclamation say?

INDEX

ABOUT THE AUTHOR

Kim Thompson lives in Columbus, Ohio, with her husband and two funny cats. She has written many books for kids. She is happy that Juneteenth is now a national holiday in the United States. Her favorite holiday is the one that is coming up next!